My
Grandma
Lives In A
Treehouse

CHRISTOPHER QUIRK & ELEONORA CALI'

If you enjoyed this book and want to know more about the author please visit @thealexanderbooks on Instagram

Other books available by Christopher Quirk

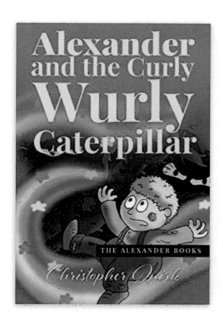 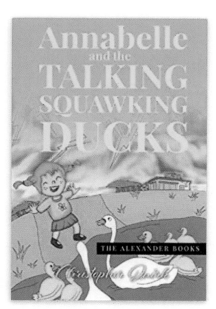

Alexander and the Curly
Wurly Caterpillar
(The Alexander Books): 1

Annabelle and the Talking
Squawking Ducks
(The Alexander Books): 2

My grandma lives in a treehouse

It's a very strange affair

Things always get rather weird

When I go over there

She lives at the bottom of my garden

It's bizarre if you ask me

The only way to get to her house

Is by climbing up a tree

She lives there with my grandad

It's really quite absurd

They're friends with all the squirrels

And have dinner with all the birds

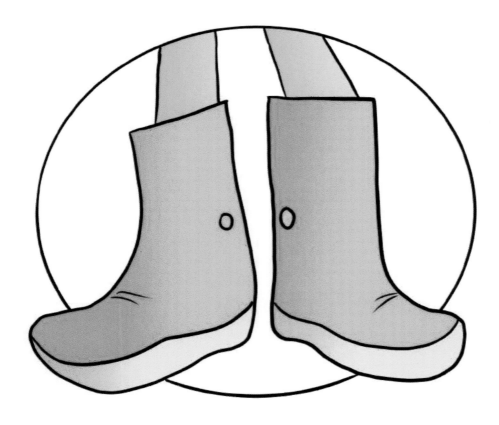

She
wears
bright
yellow
wellies

And
waterproof
cagoules

She is always jumping in puddles,
The size of swimming pools

Her treehouse isn't very big

The whole thing is made of wood

It creaks and cracks in the wind
And the furniture's just no good

But grandma
really loves it

We think she's
lost her mind

Her house is full of
acorns

Amongst the other
things we find

She's
hollowed out
the tree trunk

And in it built a slide

I see her going up and down

Her face beaming with
pride

I've often seen her out there
Swinging on a branch

Causing all the leaves to fall
In one big avalanche

Sometimes even late at night

She hoots with all the owls

Or when the moon is big and full

I hear her let out a howl

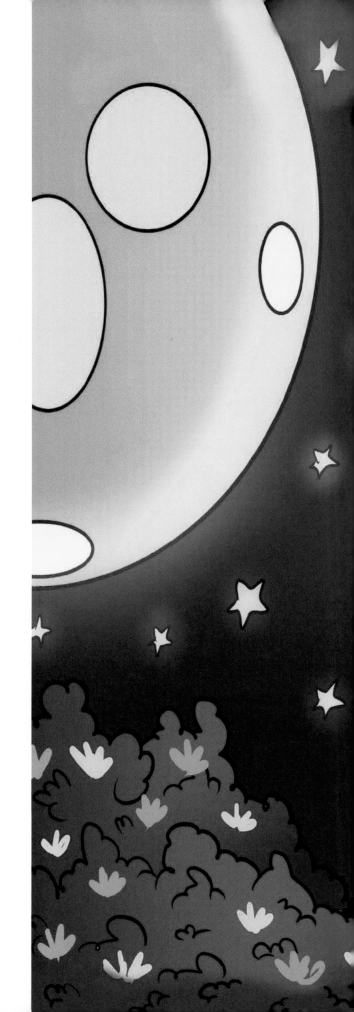

Grandma may be
a little strange

But what I love
the most

Is when she hugs
me really tight

And pulls me
really close

Her voice is really soothing
Her face is really kind

She always has time to play
She's never ever declined

My grandma lives in a treehouse

And I think you will agree

It doesn't matter where she lives

As long as she loves me

Printed in Great Britain
by Amazon